This is school

and this is Sue

and this is
Mummy Kangaroo.

The teacher's name is Mrs Drew.

She says hello to Mum and Sue.

"This is Sue," says Mrs Drew.

"Do be kind to her. She's new."

"Time to paint," says Mrs Drew.

Sue says, "I like red and blue."

moon

Balloons

"Time to glue," says Mrs Drew.

"Sue can glue a kangaroo!"

Glue

9

"Dinner time," says Mrs Drew.

"This is yummy stew," says Sue.

"Music time," says Mrs Drew.

"I can play the spoons!" says Sue.

"Home time soon," says Mrs Drew.

"But what is in your pocket, Sue?"

Sue takes out a tube of glue.

She takes some spoons and
paint out too.

"The school has rules," says Mrs Drew.

18

"You can't take those things
home with you."

Sue is sad. "Don't cry," says Prue.

"Play with them tomorrow, Sue."

"Is there school tomorrow too?"

"Is that true? Hooray!" says Sue.

23

Here is Mummy Kangaroo.
"Hi, Mum! School is cool!" says Sue.